Onwards & Upwards

Onwards & Upwards

Edited by Julian Ross

BLUEFIELD ☙ BOOKS

for Sandy and Jim,
two long-time friends
who've always enjoyed a good quote

Onwards & Upwards is published by Bluefield Books
Gr. 12, C. 9, RR 1, Winlaw, B.C., Canada V0G 2J0
1-800-296-6955

CANADIAN CATALOGUING IN PUBLICATION DATA

Main entry under title:
Onwards & upwards
Includes index.
ISBN 1-894404-00-9
1. Self-actualization (Psychology)—Quotations, maxims, etc.
2. Creative ability—Quotations, maxims, etc. I. Ross, Julian, 1952-
BF637.S4058 1999   158.1   C99-910770-4

Cover and interior design by Jim Brennan
Cover photograph © Chris Cheadle / Tony Stone Images

Printed in Canada on recycled paper

CONTENTS

CONTENTS *(continued)*

Keeping to the main road is easy, but people love to be sidetracked.　　　— Lao-tzu

🦋

If you have made mistakes, even serious ones, there is always another chance for you. What we call failure is not the falling down, but the staying down.

— Mary Pickford

🦋

Oh, be swift to love! Make haste to be kind.

— Henri Frédéric Amiel

Introduction

I've always loved a good quote, and while I can honestly say that no quote has actually changed my life, many have inspired and encouraged me for many moments, or even days, at a time.

Quotations from religious and spiritual leaders such as Mother Teresa, the Dalai Lama and Paramahansa Yogananda have been blended with quotes from entertainers, entrepreneurs, athletes and artists such as Buffy Sainte-Marie, Paul Hawken, Wayne Gretzky and Georgia O'Keefe, and I've found that many of them share surprisingly similar sentiments.

I love how a really good quote can thrill you with its truth, its ability to both provide you with something specifically pertinent to your problem or situation, as well as give you general encouragement for the long term. I hope this collection includes lots of examples to help you, as Norman Vincent Peale, and others, have said, to "keep on keeping on."

ACTION

Knowing is not enough; we must apply.
Willing is not enough; we must do.

— Johann Wolfgang von Goethe

Civilized people talk a lot and think they've done
something. We Kaispo just act.

— Chief Paiskon

Talk does not cook rice.

— Chinese proverb

In life, the great thing is to have challenges, no?

— Jacqueline Gareau

Even if you're on the right track, you'll get run over if
you just sit there.   — Will Rogers

The ultimate magic is not wishing, but doing.
— David Greer

The only joy in the world is to begin.
— Cesare Pavese

Do what you must do *when* you must do it, whether you feel like it or not.
— Brian Tracy

This chance will stand before you only once.
— Sandra Day O'Connor

The biggest sin is sitting on your ass.
— Florynce Kennedy

One chance is all you need.
— Jesse Owens

... face up to, and take the dare of the future.... That's an exciting idea to me, better than waiting with everybody else to see what happens.

— John Glenn

Action may not always bring happiness, but there is no happiness without action.

— Benjamin Disraeli

This is a world of action, and not for moping and groaning in. — Charles Dickens

You may be disappointed if you fail, but you are doomed if you don't try.

— Beverly Sills

He who hesitates is a damn fool.

— Mae West

The future begins now.

— Andrei Tarkowsky

If not now, when? If not me, who?

— Hillel

ADVICE FOR MODERN LIFE

I tell you the more I think, the more I feel that there is nothing more truly artistic than to love people.

— Vincent van Gogh

The only thing to do is to hug one's friends tight and do one's job.

— Edith Wharton

I'd rather count banana slugs in a redwood forest than browse anything on the World Wide Web.

— Clifford Stoll

It is solved by walking....

— Saint Augustine

You don't have to think about doing the right thing. If you're for the right thing, then you do it without thinking.

— Maya Angelou

It's a little embarrassing that, after 45 years of research and study, the best advice I can give is to be a little nicer to each other.

— Aldous Huxley

Dare to be naive.　　— Buckminster Fuller

In the midst of winter, I finally learned that there was in me an invincible summer. I shall tell you a great secret, my friend. Do not wait for the last judgement. It takes place every day.

— Albert Camus

This is not a dress rehearsal. This is it.

— Tom Cunningham

In the end, what affects your life most deeply are things too simple to talk about.

— Nell Blaine

Take time everyday to do something silly.

— Phillipa Walker

Life is meant to be a never-ending education, and when this is fully appreciated, we are no longer survivors but adventurers.

— David McNally

Salvation will come not through politics, which tends to separate people, but through culture, which unites them.

— Istvan Szabo

Almost anything is easier to get into than out of.

— Agnes Allen

Think for yourself and question authority.

— Timothy Leary

I'm optimistic because I see people in the face of lots of pressures still trying to meet the challenges.

— Andrew Cash

Life is like a butterfly. You can chase it, or you can let it come to you.

— Ruth Brown

... believe in life! Always human beings will live and progress to greater, broader, and fuller life.

— W.E.B. Du Bois

All I want to do is stay awake, keep my head up, prop my eyes open, with toothpicks, with trees.

— Annie Dillard

I think you should get away from competing with anything, including yourself.

— Linda Ronstadt

Everything has its astonishing, wondrous aspect, if you bring a mind to it that's really your own.

— Robertson Davies

In life, as in football, the principle to follow is — hit the line hard.   — Theodore Roosevelt

We don't know one millionth of one percent about anything.   — Thomas Edison

AGING

As we grow old, the beauty steals inward.
— Ralph Waldo Emerson

How old would you be if you didn't know how old you was?
— Satchel Paige

The secret of staying young is to live honestly, eat slowly and just not think about your age.
— Lucille Ball

We turn not older with the years but newer every day.
— Emily Dickinson

Most people say that as you get old, you have to give up things. I think you get old because you give up things.
— Theodore Francis Green

We did not change as we grew older; we just became more clearly ourselves.

— Lynn Hall

I believe that older people who have scarcely anything to lose ought to be willing to speak out on behalf of those who are young and who are subject to much greater restraint.　　　— Albert Einstein

When I dream, I am always ageless.

— Elizabeth Coatsworth

Anyone who stops learning is old, whether twenty or eighty. Anyone who keeps learning today is young. The greatest thing in life is to keep your mind young.

— Henry Ford

I'm only 49 years old. I'm still in the middle of this whole thing. I don't feel like it's finished at all. I'm still planning to write better songs.

— Paul McCartney

ANSWER LIES WITHIN

This above all: to thine own self be true,
And it must follow, as the night the day,
Thou canst not then be false to any man.

— William Shakespeare

Everybody thinks of changing humanity and nobody
thinks of changing himself.

— Leo Tolstoy

How many cares one loses when one decides not to
be something, but to be someone.

— Coco Chanel

Make it thy business to know thyself, which is the
most difficult lesson in the world.

— Miguel de Cervantes

Men go abroad to wonder at the heights of
mountains, at the huge waves of the sea, at the long

courses of the rivers, at the vast compass of the ocean, at the circular motions of the stars; and they pass by themselves without wondering.

— Saint Augustine

Know yourself. Don't accept your dog's admiration as conclusive evidence that you are wonderful.

— Ann Landers

Look within. Within is the fountain of good, and it will ever bubble up, if thou wilt ever dig.

— Marcus Aurelius

With each passage from one stage of human growth to the next we, too, must shed a protective structure. We are left exposed and vulnerable — but also yeasty and embryonic again, capable of stretching in ways we hadn't known before.

— Gail Sheehy

The only journey is the journey within.

— Rainer Maria Rilke

Often we change jobs, friends and spouses instead of ourselves. — Akbarali H. Jetha

What lies before us and what lies behind us are small matters compared to what lies within us. And when we bring what is within out into the world, miracles happen. — Henry David Thoreau

Trust yourself. You know more than you think you do. — Benjamin Spock

What comes from the heart, goes to the heart. — Samuel Taylor Coleridge

You have got to discover you, what you do, and trust it. — Barbara Streisand

Don't be sharp or flat, just be natural. — Willie Stargell

If there is any peace it will come through being, not knowing. — Henry Miller

You have to try to learn what's best for you. Let me tell you, life is not fun when you're banging your head against a brick wall all the time.

— John McEnroe

Believe nothing, no matter where you read it, or who said it, unless it agrees with your own reason and your own common sense.

— Buddha

Don't compromise yourself. You're all you've got.

— Janis Joplin

I appear to be a normal guy.... But I've always contended that the truly hip are hip on the inside.

— Dan Piraro

I'll walk where my own nature would be leading — it vexes me to choose another guide.

— Emily Brönte

Life is too fragile if your identity is solely defined by others; it is hard, a life-long task, to go on defining and redefining yourself.

— Doris Lessing

We must each find our own path and discover for ourselves the joy of being what we are.

— Laurence G. Boldt

to be nobody-but-yourself — in a world which is doing its best, night and day, to make you everybody else — means to fight the hardest battle which any human being can fight; and never stop fighting.

— e. e. cummings

If I didn't define myself for myself, I would be crunched into other people's fantasies for me and eaten alive.

— Audre Lorde

I do not live my life for the approval of others.... I try to find out what is the best, most constructive thing I can be, and to do that I answer to myself.

— William Hurt

We *are* our choices.   — Jean-Paul Sartre

Originality does not consist in saying what no one has ever said before, but in saying exactly what you think yourself.   — James Stephens

Paint what's in your head, even if you think it doesn't count — doing something that is entirely your own may be pretty interesting.

— Georgia O'Keefe

There is something in every one of you that waits and listens for the sound of the genuine in yourself. It is the only true guide you will ever have. And if you cannot hear it, you will all of your life spend your days on the ends of strings that somebody else pulls.

— Howard Thurman

If a man does not keep pace with his companions perhaps it is because he hears a different drummer. Let him step to the music he hears, however measured or far away.

— Henry David Thoreau

It took me a hundred years to figure out I can't change the world. I can only change myself. And, honey, that ain't easy, either.

— A. Elizabeth Delany

CHANGE

They always say that time changes things, but you actually have to change them yourself.

— Andy Warhol

Why do we go on doing things that we all know will harm us, perhaps irretrievably? What is the matter with us all?

— Paul Erlich

Every small, positive change we can make in ourselves repays us in confidence in the future.

— Alice Walker

The only way to make sense out of change is to plunge into it, move with it, and join the dance.

— Alan Watts

I change myself, I change the world.

— Gloria Anzaldúa

The only constant in life is change. Learn to love it and be comfortable with it. The people who succeed in the future are those who learn to walk on quicksand and dance with electrons.

— Frank Ogden

... all life... represents a risk, and the more lovingly we live our lives the more risks we take.

— M. Scott Peck

Everybody wants to be somebody; nobody wants to grow.

— Johann Wolfgang von Goethe

You're always free to change your mind and choose a different future.

— Richard Bach

Do not continue to live in the same old way. Make up your mind to do something to improve your life, and then do it. Change your consciousness; that is all that is necessary.

— Paramahansa Yogananda

COMPASSION

Try and feel, in your heart's core, the reality of others.
— Margaret Laurence

If we who have, cannot help those who have not,
then we cannot help ourselves.
— John F. Kennedy

How wonderful it is that nobody need wait a single
moment before starting to improve the world.
— Anne Frank

One of the deep secrets of life is that all that is really
worth the doing is what we do for others.
— Lewis Carroll

When I give I give myself.
— Walt Whitman

Great opportunities to help others seldom come, but small ones surround us every day.

— Sally Koch

We ourselves feel that what we are doing is just a drop in the ocean. But the ocean would be less because of that missing drop.

— Mother Teresa

I have always held firmly to the thought that each one of us can do a little to bring some portion of misery to an end.

— Albert Schweitzer

If you can't feed a hundred people, then feed just one.

— Mother Teresa

To live is not a personal thing. One has one's brothers. The contest must always be on behalf of one's brothers.

— William Saroyan

COURAGE

I once complained to my father that I didn't seem to be able to do things the same way other people did. Dad's advice? "Margo, don't be a sheep. People hate sheep. They eat sheep."

— Margo Kaufman

Never bend your head. Always hold it high. Look the world straight in the face.

— Helen Keller

When people keep telling you that you can't do a thing, you kind of like to try it.

— Margaret Chase Smith

We cannot silence the voices that we don't like hearing. We can, however, do everything in our power to make certain other voices are heard.

— Deborah Prothrow-Stith

... it's a scary process to voice your opinion voluntarily, and you have to be pretty strong to be able to do it. I don't,... yes, I do, actually, recommend it.

— k.d. lang

I think laughter may be a form of courage.... As humans we sometimes stand tall and look into the sun and laugh, and I think we are never more brave than when we do that.

— Linda Ellerbee

Be bold and courageous. When you look back on your life, you'll regret the things you didn't do more than the ones you did.

— H. Jackson Brown, Jr.

Fatigue makes cowards of us all.

— Vince Lombardi

Remember this. I can do something you can't do and you can do something I can't do. But we both have to do it.

— Mother Teresa

Independent judgement is a fairly rare quality — to learn a kind of courage to stand up for one's inner voice and to be able to say when the emperor has no clothes. — Michael Murphy

A hero is one who does what he can. The others don't. — Romain Rolland

To dare is to lose one's footing momentarily; to not dare is to lose oneself. — Søren Kierkegaard

Since we are capable of change and modifications, the future will be in many ways only as good as we have the courage to make it.

— June Tapp

Life shrinks or expands in proportion to one's courage. — Anaïs Nin

I've been absolutely terrified every moment of my life and I've never let it keep me from doing a single thing I wanted to do. — Georgia O'Keefe

Courage is being scared to death — and saddling up anyway.
— John Wayne

Pain nourishes courage. You can't be brave if you've only had wonderful things happen to you.
— Mary Tyler Moore

Anything I've ever done that ultimately was worthwhile... initially scared me to death.
— Betty Bender

Facing it — always facing it — that's the way to get through. Face it!
— Joseph Conrad

I will become a bonfire and dare the world to put me out.
— Laurence C. Boldt

What a new face courage puts on everything.
— Ralph Waldo Emerson

Our doubts are traitors and make us lose the good we oft might win by fearing to attempt.
— William Shakespeare

You can't test courage cautiously.
— Annie Dillard

We cannot wait for the world to turn, for times to change that we might change with them, for the revolution to come and carry us around in its new course. We are the future. We are the revolution.
— Beatrice Bruteau

Courage is the first of human qualities because it is a quality which guarantees the others.
— Winston Churchill

Courage is not the towering oak that sees storms come and go; it is the fragile blossom that opens in the snow.
— Alice Mackenzie Swaim

CREATIVE SPIRIT

In creating, the only hard thing's to begin.

— James Russell Lowell

I do believe it is possible to create, even without ever writing a word or painting a picture, by simply molding one's inner life. And that too is a deed.

— Etty Hillesum

Arrange whatever pieces come your way.

— Virginia Woolf

How you live your life is also art.

— Feodor Dostoevsky

One of the very worst, self-murdering lies that people tell themselves is that they are no good and have no gift and nothing important to say.

— Brenda Ueland

We all need an occasional whack on the side of the head to shake us out of routine patterns, force us to rethink problems, and stimulate us to ask new questions that may lead to other right answers.

— Roger von Oech

Thinking is easy, acting difficult, and to put one's thoughts into action, the most difficult thing in the world. — Johann Wolfgang von Goethe

I have tremendous self-doubts, all my colleagues do; we have self-doubt sessions together.

— Vladimir Ashkenazy

The thing that's important is that you never know. You're always sort of feeling your way.

— Diane Arbus

There is no end. There is no beginning. There is only the infinite passion of life.

— Federico Fellini

Nature does not ask permission. Blossom and birth whenever you feel like it.

— Clarissa Pinkola Estes

Making time for creative work is like making time for prayer.

— Jan Phillips

Art is the only way to run away without leaving home.

— Twyla Tharp

When the Spirit does not move with the hand, there is no art.

— Leonardo da Vinci

The highest purpose of art is to inspire. What else can you do? What else can you do for anyone but inspire them?

— Bob Dylan

Art washes away from the soul the dust of everyday life.

— Pablo Picasso

Never let the fear of striking out get in your way.

— Babe Ruth

The most beautiful thing we can experience is the mysterious. It is the source of all true art and science.

.— Albert Einstein

I do not try to *think* in advance. I only start to work and hope to leap a little in my spirit.

— Igor Stravinsky

You simply keep putting down one damn word after the other, as you hear them, as they come to you.

— Anne Lamott

The best time for planning a book is while you are doing the dishes.   — Agatha Christie

Great spirits have always encountered violent opposition from mediocre minds.

— Albert Einstein

Everything is gestation, then bringing forth.

— Rainer Maria Rilke

Let the beauty we love be what we do.

— Rumi

Beauty's whatever makes the adrenaline run.

— John Newlove

The voyage of discovery lies not in finding new
landscapes, but in having new eyes.

— Marcel Proust

Once I start writing there's a huge feeling of relief.
That's the playtime. That's when you are in your
sandbox.   — Ronald Bass

To be properly expressed, a thing must proceed from
within, moved by its form.

— Meister Eckhart

People are so brainwashed by the rules that they don't
know what really matters.

— Mick Jagger

The idea is to write it so that people hear it and it slides through the brain and goes straight to the heart.

— Maya Angelou

I saw the angel in the marble and I just chiseled until I set him free.   — Michelangelo

Creativity comes from trust. Trust your instinct. And never hope more than you work.

— Rita Mae Brown

To create is to make something whole from the pieces of our lives and, in the process, to become more whole ourselves, seeing with more clarity each of those pieces, understanding where they fit, how they matter.   — Jan Phillips

We do not remember days, we remember moments.

—Cesare Pavese

I have no special talents. I am only passionately curious.   — Albert Einstein

Sometimes I begin something 100 times before it takes hold and develops its own momentum.

— Sark

The "silly question" is the first intimation of some totally new development.

— Alfred North Whitehead

I don't care who likes it or who buys it. Because if you use that criterion, Mozart would never have written *Don Giovanni,* Charlie Parker would never have played anything but swing music. There comes a point at which you have to stand up and say, this is what I have to do.   — Branford Marsalis

One must avoid ambition in order to write, otherwise something else is the goal: some kind of power beyond the power of language.

— Cynthia Ozick

Each time we begin, we begin anew, alone, afraid.

— Jan Phillips

You can't wait for inspiration. You have to go after it with a club. — Jack London

I believe that each work of art, whether it is a work of great genius, or something very small, comes to the artist and says, "Here I am. Enflesh me. Give birth to me." — Madeleine L'Engle

I am afraid of losing my obscurity. Genuineness only thrives in the dark. Like celery.
— Aldous Huxley

Memory is a complicated thing, a relative to truth, but not its twin. — Barbara Kingsolver

We must overcome the notion that we must be regular. It robs us of the chance to be extraordinary and leads us to the mediocre.
— Uta Hagen

The monotony of a quiet life stimulates the creative mind. — Albert Einstein

As soon as I began painting what was in my head, the people around me were shocked.

— Leonor Fini

True art is characterized by an irresistible urge in the creative artist.

— Albert Einstein

I write in order to make sense of the business of being alive.

— Gore Vidal

I dream my painting and then I paint my dream.

— Vincent van Gogh

They come and ask me what idea I meant to embody in my Faust; as if I knew myself and could inform them.

— Johann Wolfgang von Goethe

Music attracts the angels in the universe.

— Bob Dylan

If people knew how hard I worked to get my mastery, it wouldn't seem so wonderful at all.

— Michelangelo

I don't think you can ever do your best. Doing your best is a process of *trying* to do your best.

— Townes Van Zandt

I never know when the poems will happen — they just pop out like corn in the pan.

— Allan Safarik

On some level, we are all artists, sharing the medium of life itself. Every day we add something new to the universe, bringing our human energy to the cosmic canvas.

— Jan Phillips

All the arts we practice are apprenticeship. The big art is our life.

— M.C. Richards

A hunch is creativity trying to tell you something.
— Frank Capra

Creativity is misunderstood, because the result is often given more weight than the process.
— Keith Jarrett

The way to make a mind more creative is to slow it down.
— Sam Keen

DISCIPLINE

One of the reasons I have been successful is I am well-disciplined. I have only been late three times in my life. — Dick Clark

Self-respect is the fruit of discipline; the sense of dignity grows with the ability to say no to oneself.
— Abraham Joshua Heschel

Keeping to the main road is easy, but people love to be sidetracked. — Lao-tzu

We are what we repeatedly do. Excellence, then, is not an act but a habit.
— Aristotle

When we develop the habit of plunging in without whining, complaining, or procrastinating, we are on our way to genuine freedom.
— Laurence G. Boldt

I think the one lesson I have learned is that there is no substitute for paying attention.

— Diane Sawyer

I try to be prepared for the moment, through understanding and being warmed up, knowing all about chords and scales, so I don't even have to think and I can get right to what it is I want to say.

— Pat Metheny

A life directed chiefly toward the fulfillment of personal desires sooner or later always leads to bitter disappointment.   — Albert Einstein

DO IT NOW

Nothing is so fatiguing as the eternal hanging on of an uncompleted task. — William James

Begin to be now what you will be hereafter.
— Saint Jerome

Do it for all it's worth, and do it now, and do it good.
— Roy Orbison

Seize the day and put as little trust as you can in tomorrow. — Horace

Never wait until the last minute. The last minute shall invariably cometh and goeth quicker than you thought it would. — Daniel Meacham

Begin now. Begin where you are. Begin it.
— Sark

You don't get to choose how you're going to die. Or when. You can decide how you're going to live. Now.

— Joan Baez

The time is always right to do what is right.

— Martin Luther King, Jr.

The beginning has its own power and energy. Let the buoyancy of the beginning carry you to new places!

— Sark

Most people will go to their graves with their music still inside of them.   — Benjamin Disraeli

Great is the problem of birth and death. Impermanence surrounds us. Be awake every moment. Do not waste your life.

— Buddhist text

It's helpful to look at your life and ask, "If I had one more year to live, what would I do?" We all have things we want to achieve. Don't just put them off — do them now! — John Goddard

Begin doing what you want to do now. We are not living in eternity. We have only this moment sparkling like a star in our hand — and melting like a snowflake. — Marie Beyon Ray

Things do not get better by being left alone.
— Winston Churchill

How short life is! How much I have still to do, to think and to say! We keep putting things off and meanwhile death lurks around the corner.
— Petr Ilich Tchaikovsky

Do It Yourself

As one goes through life one learns that if you don't paddle your own canoe, you don't move.

— Katharine Hepburn

My own thing is in my head. I hear sounds and if I don't get them together nobody else will.

— Jimi Hendrix

The future depends entirely on what each of us does every day.

— Gloria Steinem

Do not wait for leaders. Do it alone, person to person.

— Mother Teresa

You decide what it is you want to accomplish and then you lay out your plans to get there, and then you just do it. It's pretty straightforward.

— Nancy Ditz

Don't sit down and wait for the opportunities to come; you have to get up and make them.

— Madame C. J. Walker

The people who get on in this world are the people who get up and look for the circumstances they want, and if they can't find them, make them.

— George Bernard Shaw

Whatever there is of God and goodness in the universe, it must work itself out and express itself through us. We cannot stand aside and let God do it.

— Albert Einstein

DREAMS

Go confidently in the direction of your dreams! Live the life you've imagined. As you simplify your life, the laws of the universe will be simpler.

— Henry David Thoreau

What is now proved was once only imagined.

— William Blake

It is in our idleness, in our dreams, that the submerged truth sometimes comes to the top.

— Virginia Woolf

Those who dream by night in the dusty recesses of their minds wake in the day to find that it was vanity; but the dreamers of the day are dangerous men, for they may act their dream with open eyes, to make it possible.

— T. E. Lawrence

Dreams pass into the reality of action. From the

action stems the dream again; and this
interdependence produces the highest form of living.

— Anaïs Nin

I do not know whether I was then a man dreaming I
was a butterfly, or whether I am now a butterfly
dreaming I am a man.

— Chuang-Tse

The best way to make your dreams come true is to
wake up. — Paul Valery

If you don't have a wild dream, you'll never try and
you'll never get and you'll never achieve.

— Celia Franca

Dreams are true while they last, and do we not live in
dreams? — Alfred, Lord Tennyson

Nothing happens unless first a dream.

— Carl Sandburg

Dreams and dedication are a powerful combination.

— William Longgood

Go confidently in the directions of your dreams. Act as though it were impossible to fail.

— Dorothea Brandt

Don't be afraid of the space between your dreams and reality. If you can dream it, you can make it so.

— Belva Davis

ENJOY THE MOMENT

Hold out your hands and feel the luxury of the sunshine.   — Helen Keller

Life moves pretty fast; you don't stop and look around every once in a while, you could miss it.
                    — John Hughes

When we get too caught up in the busyness of the world, we lose connection with one another — and ourselves.   — Jack Kornfield

Paradise is where I am.   — Voltaire

Go slowly, breathe and smile.
                    — Thich Nhat Hanh

Be absolutely determined to enjoy what you do.
                    — Gerry Sikorski

You have to sniff out joy. Keep your nose to the joy trail.
— Buffy Sainte-Marie

But it's morning. Within my hands is another day. Another day to listen and love and walk and glory. I am here for another day.
— Hugh Prather

How we spend our days is, of course, how we spend our lives.
— Annie Dillard

Every day I wake up, I think, what a blessing — I'm alive. I don't care if it snows, it rains, it thunderstorms — a heatwave. I think, I'm here — this is terrific!
— Richard Harris

Every day is a renewal, every morning the daily miracle. This joy you feel is life.
— Gertrude Stein

Look, children, hailstones! Let's rush out!
— Basho

ENTHUSIASM

Life begets life. Energy creates energy. It is by
spending oneself that one becomes rich.

— Sarah Bernhardt

Put a grain of boldness into everything you do.

— Baltasar Gracian

Nothing great was ever achieved without enthusiasm.

— Ralph Waldo Emerson

This world belongs to the energetic.

— Ralph Waldo Emerson

You will do foolish things, but do them with
enthusiasm.   — Colette

Enthusiasm is the most beautiful word on earth.

— Christian Morgenstern

Practice being excited. — Bill Foster

Energy and persistence conquer all things.
— Benjamin Franklin

All we need to make us really happy is something to
be enthusiastic about. — Charles Kingsley

Plunge boldly into the thick of life!
— Johann Wolfgang von Goethe

FAILURE / FEAR

You're gonna lose some ballgames and you're gonna win some ballgames, and that's about it.

— Sparky Anderson

Nothing in life is to be feared. It is only to be understood.　　　　— Marie Curie

Failure is not failure but the opportunity to begin again... more intelligently.

— Henry Ford

When we can begin to take our failures non-seriously, it means we are ceasing to be afraid of them. It is of immense importance to learn to *laugh at ourselves*.

— Katherine Mansfield

I have not failed. I have successfully discovered twelve hundred ideas that don't work.

— Thomas Edison

What is there to be afraid of? The worst thing that can happen is you fail. So what? I failed at a lot of things. My first record was horrible.

— John Mellancamp

There is no failure except in no longer trying.

— Elbert Hubbard

If you have made mistakes, even serious ones, there is always another chance for you. What we call failure is not the falling down, but the staying down.

— Mary Pickford

A person's errors are his portals of discovery.

— James Joyce

Failure? I never encountered it. All I ever met were temporary setbacks.   — Dottie Watters

GETTING STARTED

The gods send thread for the web begun.
>— Leif Smith

Begin somewhere; you cannot build a reputation on what you intend to do.
>— Liz Smith

What you will do, matters. All you need is to do it.
>— Judy Grahn

Only begin and then the mind grows heated. Only begin and the task will be completed.
>— Johann Wolfgang von Goethe

Set out from any point. They are all alike. They all lead to a point of departure.
>— Antonio Porchia

The great composer does not set to work because he is inspired, but becomes inspired because he is working. Beethoven, Wagner, Bach and Mozart settled down day after day to the job in hand with as much regularity as an accountant settles down each day to his figures. They didn't waste time waiting for inspiration.

— Ernest Newman

GOALS

My career is a testimony that if you stick to your goals and integrity, appreciation and acceptance will eventually come.   — Bonnie Raitt

My mission on earth is to recognize the void — inside and outside of me — and fill it!

— Elie Wiesel

If you want to live a happy life, tie it to a goal, not to people or things.   — Albert Einstein

Establishing goals is all right if you don't let them deprive you of interesting detours.

— Doug Larson

Goals are dreams with deadlines.

— Diana Scharf Hunt

If you don't know where you're going, you will wind up somewhere else.　— Yogi Berra

Shoot for the moon! If you miss, you'll land among the stars.　— Les Brown

Keep high aspirations, moderate expectations, and small needs.　— H. Stein

Even though we think of the goal as some future state to achieve, the real goal is always the life of this moment.

— Charlotte Joko Beck

If you don't always strive toward new goals, you lose vitality. That is disastrous.

— Shigeki Tashiro

GRATITUDE

Sometimes I go about in pity for myself, and all the while a great wind is bearing me across the sky.

— Ojibway saying

Feeling gratitude and not expressing it is like wrapping a present and not giving it.

— William Arthur Ward

There are hundreds of ways to kneel and kiss the ground. — Rumi

What a wonderful life I've had! I only wish I'd realized it sooner. — Colette

Be glad for life because it gives you the chance to love and to work and to look up at the stars.

— Henry Van Dyke

I thank You God for this most amazing day; for the leaping greenly spirits of trees and a blue true dream of sky; and for everything which is natural which is infinite which is yes.   — e.e. cummings

Most human beings have an almost infinite capacity for taking things for granted.

— Aldous Huxley

If the only prayer you say in your whole life is "Thank you," that would suffice.

— Meister Eckhart

HAPPINESS

Happiness not in another place, but in this place....
Not for another hour, but this hour.

— Walt Whitman

Happiness consists in activity — it is a running
stream and not a stagnant pool.

— Good

Learn to let go. That is the key to happiness.

— Buddha

Satisfaction of one's curiosity is one of the greatest
sources of happiness in life.

— Linus Pauling

We all live with the objective of being happy; our
lives are all different and yet the same.

— Anne Frank

Most folks are about as happy as they make up their minds to be. — Abraham Lincoln

It is only possible to live happily ever after on a day-to-day basis. — Margaret Bonnano

Why not seize the pleasure at once? How often is happiness destroyed by preparation, foolish preparation? — Jane Austen

One is happy as a result of one's own efforts — once one knows the necessary ingredients of happiness — simple tastes, a certain degree of courage, self-denial to a point, love of work, and, above all, a clear conscience. — George Sand

Happiness is when what you think, what you say, and what you do are in harmony.
— Mahatma Gandhi

I know well that happiness is in little things.
— John Ruskin

He who bends to himself a Joy
Doth the wingèd life destroy;
But he who kisses the Joy as it flies
Lives in Eternity's sunrise.

— William Blake

If you want to be happy, be.

— Leo Tolstoy

IDEAS & IMAGINATION

Why is it I get my best ideas in the morning while I am shaving? — Albert Einstein

Nighttime is really the best time to work. All the ideas are there to be yours because everyone else is asleep.
— Catherine O'Hara

Imagination means letting the birds in one's head out of their cages and watching them fly up in the air.
— Gerald Brenan

If you don't daydream and kind of plan things out in your imagination, you never get there. So you have to start someplace. — Robert Duvall

The way to have good ideas is to have a lot of ideas and throw away the bad ones.
— Linus Pauling

The man who has no imagination has no dreams.
— Muhammad Ali

The future is what you dream.
— Morris West

Imagination is the highest kite that one can fly.
— Lauren Bacall

Why, sometimes I've believed as many as six
impossible things before breakfast.
— Lewis Carroll

Few people have the imagination for reality.
— Johann Wolfgang von Goethe

When I examine myself and my methods of thought,
I come close to the conclusion that the gift of fantasy
(imagination) has meant more to me than my talent
for absorbing absolute knowledge.
— Albert Einstein

Ideas won't keep. Something must be done with them.
— Alfred North Whitehead

To stay ahead, always have your next idea waiting in the wings.
— Rosabeth Moss Kanter

Imagination is more important than information.
— Robert Fulghum

Imagination is more important than knowledge.
— Albert Einstein

The opportunities of man are limited only by his imagination. But so few have imagination that there are ten thousand fiddlers to one composer.
— Charles F. Kettering

He turns not back who is bound to a star.
— Leonardo da Vinci

When I am completely myself, entirely alone, and of good cheer — it is on such occasions that my ideas flow best and most abundantly.

— Wolfgang Amadeus Mozart

Ideas, like wind-blown seeds, have a way of crossing boundaries and appearing in unlikely places.

— William Irving Thompson

All good ideas have already been thought; the point is to try and think them again.

— Johann Wolfgang von Goethe

Your imagination is your preview of life's coming attractions.

— Albert Einstein

Ideas are like rabbits. You get a couple and learn how to handle them, and pretty soon you have a dozen.

— John Steinbeck

I thought you could thrash, beat, pummel an idea into existence. Under such treatment, of course, any decent idea folds up its paws, fixes its eyes on eternity, and dies. — Ray Bradbury

So you see the imagination needs moodling: long, inefficient, happy idling, dawdling and puttering.
— Brenda Ueland

INTERCONNECTEDNESS

For behind all seen things lies something vaster;
everything is but a path, a portal, a window opening
on something more than itself.

— Antoine de Saint-Exupéry

These are dangerous times for the Earth. We must get
back to nature... through the application of both
science and philosophy.

— Prince Charles

After all, the earth does not need humans to survive,
but we need the earth.   — Derek Elsom

Man did not weave the web of life, he is merely a
strand in it. Whatever he does to the web, he does to
himself.   — Chief Seattle

Remember that you are all people and that all people
are you.   — Joy Harjo

It seems ridiculous to have divisive things going on anywhere in the world.

— Roberta Bondar

Everyone thinks about the parts of their life, no one thinks of the whole.   — Seneca

Integrate what you believe into every single area of your life.   — Meryl Streep

If the entire is to feed your soul, then in the littlest you must see the whole.

— Johann Wolfgang von Goethe

This we know. All things are connected like the blood which unites one family. All things are connected.

— Chief Seattle

Until mankind can extend the circle of his compassion to include all living things he will never, himself, know peace.   — Albert Schweitzer

When we try to pick out anything by itself, we find it hitched to everything else in the universe.

— John Muir

I feel myself so much a part of everything living that I am not in the least concerned with the beginning or ending of the concrete existence of any one person in this eternal flow.　　　— Albert Einstein

When the green woods laugh with the voice of joy.

— William Blake

The faintness of the stars, the freshness of the morning, the dewdrop on the flower, speaks to me.

— Chief Dan George

The sun, with all the planets revolving around it and depending on it, can still ripen a bunch of grapes as though it had nothing else in the universe to do.

— Galileo

INTUITION

Even when all the experts agree, they may well be mistaken.
— Bertrand Russell

The heart makes better decisions than the head and it doesn't keep you awake at night doing it — just announces one day what the decision is.
— Miles Morland

Trust your hunches. They're usually based on facts filed away just below the conscious level.
— Dr. Joyce Brothers

I call intuition cosmic fishing. You feel the nibble, and then you have to hook the fish.
— Buckminster Fuller

It is by logic that we prove, but by intuition that we discover.
— Henri Poincaré

Keep On Keeping On

One of the simplest things about all the facts of life is that to get where you want to go, you must keep on keeping on. — Norman Vincent Peale

Don't give up trying to do what you really want to do. Where there is love and inspiration I don't think you can go wrong. — Ella Fitzgerald

Persistence is not a long race; it is many short races one after another. — Walter Elliott

The way I see it, if you want the rainbow, you gotta put up with the rain. — Dolly Parton

Sometimes you have to play for a long time to be able to play like yourself. — Miles Davis

I have discovered in life that there are ways of getting

almost anywhere you want to go, if you really want to go.

— Langston Hughes

Great works are performed not by strength but by perseverance.   — Samuel Johnson

Never give up. Never, never, never, never give up.

— Winston Churchill

It ain't over till it's over, and even then it's not over!

— Jesse Jackson

A successful entrepreneur backs his own ideas, then gets off his butt and makes them work. Persistence is the most important thing.

— Richard Price

I don't think of myself as a symbol of the Sixties, but I do think of myself as a symbol — of following through on your beliefs.

— Joan Baez

God gave me the stubbornness of a mule and a fairly keen scent. — Albert Einstein

I am not the smartest or most talented person in the world, but I succeeded because I keep going, and going, and going. — Sylvester Stallone

I realized early on that success was tied to not giving up.... If you simply didn't give up, you would outlast the people who came in on the bus with you.

— Harrison Ford

KINDNESS

My religion is very simple — my religion is kindness.

— The Dalai Lama

A little kindness from person to person is better than a vast love for all humankind.

— Richard Dehmel

Life is short and we never have enough time for gladdening the hearts of those who travel the way with us. Oh, be swift to love! Make haste to be kind.

— Henri Frédéric Amiel

Kind words can be short and easy to speak, but their echoes are truly endless.

— Mother Teresa

Kindness can become its own motive. We are made kind by being kind.   — Eric Hoffer

Let us open up our natures, throw wide the doors of our hearts and let in the sunshine of goodwill and kindness.   — O.S. Marden

Two important things are: to have a genuine interest in people and to be kind to them. Kindness, I've discovered, is everything in life.

—Isaac Bashevis Singer

Always be a little kinder than necessary.

— James M. Barrie

LIFE

The purpose of life, after all, is to live it, to taste experience to the utmost, to reach out eagerly and without fear for newer and richer experiences.

— Eleanor Roosevelt

Be cheerful while you are alive.

— Ptahhotpe

If you ask me what I came to do in this world, I, an artist, will answer you: I am here to live out loud.

— Emile Zola

Warm, eager, living life — to be rooted in life — to learn, to desire to know, to feel, to think, to act. That is what I want. — Katherine Mansfield

All are but parts of one stupendous whole,
Whose body nature is, and God the soul.

— Alexander Pope

I like living. I have sometimes been wildly, despairingly, acutely miserable, racked with sorrow, but through it all I still know quite certainly that just to *be* alive is a grand thing.

— Agatha Christie

Only a life lived for others is a life worthwhile.

— Albert Einstein

There is no cure for birth and death save to enjoy the interval.

— George Santayana

Life is either a daring adventure or nothing. To keep our faces toward change and behave like free spirits in the presence of fate is strength undefeatable.

— Helen Keller

Life is what we make it; always has been, always will be.

— Grandma Moses

I finally figured out the only reason to be alive is to enjoy it.

— Rita Mae Brown

LIFELONG LEARNING

Education is not the filling of a pail, but the lighting of a fire. — William Butler Yeats

I am convinced that it is of primordial importance to learn more every year than the year before.
— Peter Ustinov

To be able to be caught up in the world of thought — that is to be educated. — Edith Hamilton

A great part of the information I have was acquired by looking up something and finding something else on the way. — Franklin Adams

Help conquer the IQ shortage. Worry less and think more. — Robert Anton Wilson

Everything has been figured out except how to live.

— Jean-Paul Sartre

Knowledge is the key that unlocks all the doors. It doesn't matter what you look like or where you come from if you have knowledge.

— Benjamin S. Carson

... that is what learning is. You suddenly understand something you've understood all your life, but in a new way.

— Doris Lessing

The mind, once expanded to the dimensions of larger ideas, never returns to its original size.

— Oliver Wendell Holmes

Human history becomes more and more a race between education and catastrophe.

— H.G. Wells

To learn is to change. Education is a process that changes the learner.

— George Leonard

The important thing is not to stop questioning.
— Albert Einstein

I didn't need no diploma to do what I can do.
— Louis Armstrong

In the case of good books, the point is not to see how many of them you can get through, but rather how many can get through to you.
— Mortimer J. Adler

The best-educated human being is the one who understands most about the life in which he is placed.
— Helen Keller

A primary duty of education is to let curiosity rip.
— Ivor Brown

L O V E

Let us always meet each other with a smile, for the smile is the beginning of love.

> — Mother Teresa

There is a single magic, a single power, a single salvation, and a single happiness — and that is called loving.

> — Herman Hesse

Perhaps the chief business of life is simply to learn how to love.

> — Marsha Sinetar

It is not a matter of thinking much but of loving much — so do whatever most kindles love in you.

> — Saint Teresa

We love because it's the only true adventure.

> — Nikki Giovanni

Let there be spaces in your togetherness
And let the winds of the heavens dance between you.

— Kahlil Gibran

All you need is love, love is all you need. Yes, I still
believe that and I'm sticking to it.

— George Harrison

Love, and do what you will.

— Saint Augustine

The giving of love is an education in itself.

— Eleanor Roosevelt

I believe that unarmed truth and unconditional love
will have the final word in reality.

— Martin Luther King, Jr.

Love is the highest, the grandest, the most inspiring,
the most sublime principle in creation.

— Paramahansa Yogananda

True love begins when nothing is looked for in
return.   — Antoine de Saint-Exupéry

Love is a fruit in season at all times, and within the
reach of every hand.   — Mother Teresa

Sometimes it's a form of love just to talk to somebody
that you have nothing in common with and still be
fascinated by their presence.
                              — David Byrne

What happiness to be beloved; and O, what bliss, ye
gods, to love.   — Johann Wolfgang von Goethe

Love doesn't just sit there, like a stone; it has to be
made, like bread, remade all the time, made new.
                              — Ursula K. LeGuin

In our life there is a single colour, as on an artist's
palette, which provides the meaning of life and art. It
is the colour of love.   — Marc Chagall

What the world really needs is more love and less paperwork.   — Pearl Bailey

We can do no great things, only small things with great love.   —Mother Teresa

It is only with the heart that one can see rightly; what is essential is invisible to the eye.

— Antoine de Saint-Exupéry

And yet, a single night of universal love could save everything.   — Roland Giguere

MORE ADVICE
FOR MODERN LIFE

Always go to the bathroom when you have a chance.
— King George V

Angels fly because they take themselves lightly.
— G.K. Chesterton

There is more to life than increasing its speed.
— Mahatma Gandhi

Dwell as near as possible to the channel in which
your life flows.   — Henry David Thoreau

No matter how big or soft or warm your bed is, you
still have to get out of it.
— Grace Slick

When I'm pushing myself, testing myself, that's when I'm happiest. That's when the rewards are greatest.

— Sissy Spacek

If a person can laugh, particularly at himself, he can probably step back and get the right perspective on things.

— William Gold

Joy will find a way.

— Bruce Cockburn

Decide to network. Use every letter you write, every conversation you have, every meeting you attend to express your fundamental beliefs and dreams.

— Robert Muller

Done is better than perfect.

— Anne Mollegen Smith

With every true friendship we build more firmly the foundations on which the peace of the world rests.

— Mahatma Gandhi

Think of all the beauty still left around you and be happy. — Anne Frank

The important things in life cannot be gotten in advance. They must be gathered every day.
— George Regas

I've got my faults, but living in the past isn't one of them — there's no future in it.
— Sparky Anderson

The important thing is this: to be able at any moment to sacrifice what we are for what we could become.
— Charles Du Bos

One of the secrets of a long and fruitful life is to forgive everybody everything every night before you go to bed. — Ann Landers

In wisdom gathered over time I have found that every experience is a form of exploration.
— Ansel Adams

Feelings are everywhere — be gentle.

— J. Masai

You must learn day by day, year by year, to broaden your horizon. The more things you love, the more you are interested in, the more you enjoy, the more you are indignant about — the more you have left when anything happens.

— Ethel Barrymore

Life is like a ten-speed bike. Most of us have gears we never use.

— Charles M. Schulz

There must be more to life than having everything.

— Maurice Sendak

We should tackle reality in a slightly joking way... otherwise we miss its point.

— Lawrence Durrell

I never worry about falling when I'm going for a win.

— Todd Brooker

The ideals which have lighted my way, and time after time have given me new courage to face life cheerfully, have been Kindness, Beauty, and Truth.

— Albert Einstein

Money mon-monee!... If numbers is where you get your kicks from — to have plenty — then you're lost. Because it don't have no end.

— Bob Marley

If you don't like the way the world is, you change it. You have an obligation to change it. You just do it one step at a time.   — Marian Wright Edelman

A musician must make his music, an artist must paint, a poet must write if he is to ultimately be at peace with himself.   — Abraham Maslow

That is how the world works — not like an arrow, but a boomerang.   — Ralph Ellison

I believe that a simple and unassuming life is good for everybody, physically and mentally.

— Albert Einstein

For fast-acting relief, try slowing down.

— Lily Tomlin

If someone said, "Write a sentence about your life," I'd write, "I want to go outside and play."

— Jenna Elfman

There is no pillow so soft as a clear conscience.

— French proverb

All we do is make plans. We think that somewhere there are going to be green pastures. It's crazy. Listen — *now* is good. *Now* is wonderful.

— Mel Brooks

I will always have the courage to say what I want.
— Fiona Apple

The art of living consists in knowing which impulses to obey and which must be made to obey.
— Sydney J. Harris

NATURE

Ho, weary town worker, come to the woods and rest.

— John Muir

Learn to pause or nothing worthwhile will catch up to you.

— D. King

There's music in the waking woods. There's glory in the air.

— John Clare

I get a wonderful peace and the most exquisite pleasure from my friendship with the stars.

— Ellen Glasgow

Look deep, deep into nature, and then you will understand everything better.

— Albert Einstein

Afoot and light-hearted I take to the open road;
Healthy, free, the world before me.
                              — Walt Whitman

Beauty breaks in everywhere.
                              — Ralph Waldo Emerson

Spring has returned. The earth is like a child that
knows poems.   — Rainer Maria Rilke

The arch of sky and mightiness of storms have moved
the spirit within me, till I am carried away trembling
with joy.   — Uvavnuk

The world is too much with us; late and soon,
Getting and spending, we lay waste our powers;
Little we see in Nature that is ours....
                              — William Wordsworth

I'd rather wake up in the middle of nowhere than in
any city on earth.   — Steve McQueen

The wind into which I am climbing is fragrant of beyonds and distances, of watersheds and foreign languages, of mountains and southern places. It is full of promise. — Hermann Hesse

Today I have grown taller from walking with the trees. — Karle W. Baker

There is something infinitely healing in the repeated strains of nature — the assurance that dawn comes after night, and spring after winter.
— Rachel Carson

We are nature. We are nature seeing nature. The red-winged blackbird flies in us.
— Susan Griffin

Flowers... have a mysterious and subtle influence upon the feelings, not unlike some strains of music. They relax the tenseness of the mind. They dissolve its rigor. — Henry Ward Beecher

ONWARDS & UPWARDS

Everyone has, inside... what shall I call it? A piece of good news! Everyone... is a great, very important character. — Ugo Betti

Noble deeds and hot baths are the best cures for depression. —Dodie Smith

I'm not afraid of storms, for I'm learning how to sail my ship. — Louisa May Alcott

What we've got to do is to keep up our spirits and be neighborly. — Charles Dickens

I think these difficult times have helped me to understand how infinitely rich and beautiful life is, and that so many things one worries about are of no importance whatsoever. — Isak Dinesen

When down in the mouth, remember Jonah — he came out all right. — Thomas Edison

It is a common experience that a problem difficult at night is resolved in the morning after the committee of sleep has worked on it.
— John Steinbeck

... the vibrations of good thoughts are never lost, but are a quiet stimulus of joy and well-being...
— Paramahansa Yogananda

Turn your face to the sun and the shadows fall behind you. — Maori proverb

In knowing how to overcome little things, a centimetre at a time, gradually when bigger things come, you're prepared. — Katherine Dunham

There is time for everything.
— Thomas Edison

... at the bottom of the abyss comes the voice of salvation. The black moment is the moment when the real message of transformation is going to come. At the darkest comes the light.

— Joseph Campbell

Ex-pression is the opposite of de-pression. When we de-press, we usually need to ex-press. Tune your channel to creativity and let the goodness flow out of you.   — Sark

Break out into blithe, merry song when you feel an attack of the blues pressing on; take up some book of noble prose or verse and 'lend to the rhyme of the poet the beauty of thy voice'; or chatter with your nearest companion in a sprightly strain — and you will melt imperceptibly into the mood you have counterfeited.   — Sara A. Hubbard

When your heart speaks, take good notes.
                     — Judith Campbell

If lots more of us loved each other, we'd solve lots more problems. And then the world would be a *gasser*. — Louis Armstrong

I have learned to live each day as it comes, and not to borrow trouble by dreading tomorrow. It is the dark menace of the future that makes cowards of us. — Dorothy Dix

Life likes to be taken by the lapel and told: "I am with you kid. Let's go." — Maya Angelou

Challenges make you discover things about yourself that you never really knew. They're what make the instrument stretch, what make you go beyond the norm. — Cicely Tyson

There is no such thing as a great talent without great willpower. — Honoré de Balzac

Just do your best today and tomorrow will come...
tomorrow's going to be a busy day, a happy day.
— Helen Boehm

(We need to) leave time in our day for being deep,
reflective people who appreciate the sun coming up
and going down, and who cherish each other.
— Bo Lozoff

And above everything else, let the deep dream of
peace make us all bold, and let us all be bold on
behalf of peace.   — Candas Jane Dorsey

I think in terms of the day's resolutions, not the
year's.   — Henry Moore

By not listening to yourself, you deny yourself
tremendous possibilities and glorious opportunity.
— Steven Spielberg

Every child, every person needs to know that they are a source of joy; every child, every person needs to be accepted.

— Jean Vanier

Patience is needed with everyone, but first of all with ourselves.

— Saint Francis de Sales

I always entertain great hopes.

— Robert Frost

Rest is not a matter of doing absolutely nothing. Rest is repair.

— Daniel W. Joselyn

No task is a long one but the task on which one dare not start. It becomes a nightmare.

— Charles Baudelaire

If I feel strongly, I say it. I know I can do more good by being vocal than by staying quiet.

— Martina Navratilova

Inside myself is a place where I live alone, and that's where you renew your springs that never dry up.

— Pearl S. Buck

One of the most tragic things I know about human nature is that all of us tend to put off living. We are all dreaming of some magical rose garden over the horizon — instead of enjoying the roses that are blooming outside our window today.

— Dale Carnegie

What's the use of worrying? It never was worthwhile, So, pack up your troubles in your old kit-bag, And smile, smile, smile.

— George Asaf

I find ecstasy in living; the mere essence of living is joy enough.   — Emily Dickinson

It's 5% talent, 15% skill, and 80% hanging in there.

— Lucy Lawless

What you can't get out of, get into wholeheartedly.

— Mignon McLaughlin

Start by doing what's necessary, then what's possible and suddenly you are doing the impossible.

— Saint Francis of Assisi

There is nothing inevitable. The actions of the past operate at every instant and so, at every instant, does freedom.

— Nan Shin

In the end we shall have had enough of cynicism and scepticism and humbug and we shall want to live more musically.

— Vincent van Gogh

In a very real sense, we are the authors of our own lives.

— Mandy Aftel

Don't even make a list. Do everything right now.

— Sigourney Weaver

I don't want to get to the end of my life and find that I lived just the length of it. I want to have lived the width of it as well.   — Diane Ackerman

When the first baby laughed for the first time, the laugh broke into a thousand pieces and they all went skipping about, and that was the beginning of fairies.
— James M. Barrie

All walking is discovery. On foot we take the time to see things whole.   — Hal Borland

Life is playfulness.... We need to play so that we can discover the magic all around us.
— Flora Colao

Be bold. If you're going to make an error, make a doozey, and don't be afraid to hit the ball.
— Billie Jean King

This Saturday, do something you have wanted to do for years. Something just for yourself. And repeat this process once a month.

— Denis Waitely

You miss 100% of the shots you never take.

— Wayne Gretzky

There is no elevator to success. It's just stairs. I've tripped on those stairs a couple of times, but I'm still climbing.

— Bryan Fogarty

... celebrate the good, the simple, the modest, the truthful, because that's what lasts forever.

— Fred Rogers

Just go out there and do what you have to do.

— Martina Navratilova

Every time I catch myself saying, "Oh no, you shouldn't try that," I think, "Yes, I *should*."

— Erica Jong

I've always believed that you can think positive just as well as you can think negative.

— Sugar Ray Robinson

I may not be totally perfect, but parts of me are excellent.

— Ashleigh Brilliant

Joy in the universe, and keen curiousity about it all — that has been my religion.

— John Burroughs

I just took the energy it takes to pout and wrote some blues.

— Duke Ellington

It's a good thing to have all the props pulled out from under us occasionally. It gives us some sense of what is rock under our feet, and what is sand.

— Madeleine L'Engle

Attitude will take you further than talent.

— Ruthie Bolton-Holifield

Too many people, too many demands, too much to do; competent, busy, hurrying people. It just isn't living at all. — Anne Morrow Lindberg

Time you enjoy wasting, is not wasted.
— John Lennon

Look for the truth. It wants to be found.
— Blaise Pascal

Each one of us has a fire in our heart for something. It's our goal in life to find it and keep it lit.
— Mary Lou Retton

The one serious conviction that a person should have is that nothing should be taken too seriously.
— N.M. Butler

Heaven and hell is right now.... You make it heaven or you make it hell by your actions.
— George Harrison

It has been said that no person ever sank under the burden of the day. But it's when tomorrow's burden is added to the burden of today that the weight becomes unbearable. Never load yourselves so, my friends.

— George MacDonald

Rest is not idleness, and to lie sometimes on the grass under the trees on a summer's day, listening to the murmur of the water, or watching the clouds float across the sky, is by no means a waste of time.

— Sir J. Lubbock

It's never too late — in fiction or in life — to revise.

— Nancy Thayer

Opportunity

Too often the opportunity knocks, but by the time you push back the chain, push back the bolt, unhook the two locks and shut off the burglar alarm, it's too late. — Rita Coolidge

Opportunity follows struggle. It follows effort. It follows hard work. It doesn't come before.
— Shelby Steele

Opportunities are like pole beans. You have to keep picking them so more can grow.
— Hope Wallis

I happened on the idea of fitting an engine to a bicycle simply because I did not want to ride crowded trains and buses. — Soichire Honda

Your success in life does not altogether depend on ability and training; it also depends on your determination to grasp opportunities that are presented to you. — Paramahansa Yogananda

One can never consent to creep when one has an impulse to soar. — Helen Keller

Forget failures. Forget mistakes. Forget everything except what you're going to do now and do it. Today is your lucky day. — Will Durant

Why, then the world's mine oyster,
Which I with sword will open.
— William Shakespeare

PATIENCE

Nothing can be rushed. Things must grow, they must grow upward....   — Paul Klee

Far away there in the sunshine are my highest aspirations. I may not reach them, but I can look up and see their beauty, believe in them and try to follow their lead.   — Louisa May Alcott

The key to everything is patience. You get the chicken by hatching the egg, not by smashing it.
    — Arnold H. Glasow

There's a fine line between fishing and standing on the shore like an idiot.
    — Steven Wright

POWER OF THE MIND

If you believe you have power, that gives you power, and if you use it, act on it, you can make things happen.   — Maxine Walters

You can have anything you want if you want it desperately enough. You must want it with an inner exuberance that erupts through the skin and joins the energy that created the world.

— Sheila Graham

No one knows what he can do until he tries.

— Syrus

You *can* do what you have to do, and sometimes you can do it even better than you think you can.

— Jimmy Carter

They are able who think they are able.

— Virgil

One comes to be of just such stuff as that on which the mind is set. — Upanishads

The most powerful weapon on earth is the human soul on fire. — Ferdinand Foch

We become what we contemplate.
— Plato

The very act of seeking sets something in motion to meet us; something in the universe or in the unconscious responds as if to an invitation.
— Jean Shinoda Bolen

If you think you can, or you can't, you're right.
— Henry Ford

Nothing in this world is so powerful as an idea whose time has come. — Victor Hugo

Nothing is impossible, unless you think it is.
— Paramahansa Yogananda

Whatever we believe about ourselves and our ability
comes true for us.   — Susan L. Taylor

By our thinking, we create our individual and collec-
tive experience of reality. Changing our thinking for
the better improves the quality of our own lives, and
in so doing, uplifts all around us.
— Laurence G. Boldt

The greatest discovery of my generation is that human
beings can alter their lives by altering their attitudes
of mind.   — William James

The universe is change; our life is what our thoughts
make it.   — Marcus Aurelius

You give birth to that on which you fix your mind.
— Antoine de Saint-Exupéry

We are what we think. All that we are arises with our thoughts. With our thoughts we make the world.

— Buddha

Men imagine that thought can be kept secret, but it cannot; it rapidly crystallizes into habit, and habit solidifies into circumstance.

— James Allen

For one who has conquered the mind, the mind is the best of friends. But for one who has failed to do so, his very mind will be his greatest enemy.

— Bhagavad-Gita

It is our duty as men and women to proceed as though limits to our abilities do not exist.

— Pierre Teilhard de Chardin

I am flesh and blood. But my mind is the focus of much lightning.

— Allen Ginsberg

If you are possessed by an idea, you find it expressed everywhere, you even *smell* it.

— Thomas Mann

I'm convinced that 85 percent of your capacity is mental.

— Guy Lafleur

I have found that if you love life, life will love you back.

— Arthur Rubinstein

Right Action

If at the beginning and end of our lives we depend upon others' kindness, why then in the middle should we not act kindly to others?

— The Dalai Lama

I really don't see the point in creating anything if you aren't also trying to make the world a better place.

— Buffy Sainte-Marie

What you do may seem insignificant, but it's very important that you do it.

— Mahatma Gandhi

Everybody, sooner or later, sits down to a banquet of consequences.

— Robert Louis Stevenson

We have to do the best we can. This is our sacred human responsibility. — Albert Einstein

SELF-WORTH

Whatever you want in life, other people are going to want, too. Believe in yourself enough to accept the idea that you have an equal right to it.

— Diane Sawyer

We have to learn to be our own best friends because we fall too easily into the trap of being our worst enemies.

— Roderick Thorp

No one can make you feel inferior without your consent.

— Eleanor Roosevelt

A human being's first responsibility is to shake hands with himself.

— Henry Winkler

SIMPLICITY

Our life is frittered away by detail.... Simplify, simplify.
— Henry David Thoreau

Life is not complex. We are complex. Life is simple, and the simple thing is the right thing.
— Oscar Wilde

Simplicity is the ultimate sophistication.
— Leonardo da Vinci

I stopped opening my mail and now my life is so much simpler.
— Albert Einstein

SOLITUDE

Do not the most moving moments of our life find us
without words?   — Marcel Marceau

My heart leaps up when I behold
        A rainbow in the sky:
        So was it when my life began;
        So is it now I am a man;
        So be it when I shall grow old,
        Or let me die!   — William Wordsworth

After silence, that which comes nearest to expressing
the inexpressible is music.
                        — Aldous Huxley

What a lovely surprise to finally discover how
unlonely being alone can be.
                    — Ellen Burstyn

Success

Knowing what you want is your first step. You have to get some momentum up and then success breeds success. — Bill Murray

Most success comes from ignoring the obvious. — Trevor Holdsworth

Whenever you see a successful business, someone once made a courageous decision. — Peter Drucker

Chance is always powerful. Let your hook be always cast; in the pool where you least expect it, there will be a fish. — Ovid

Devote your entire will power to mastering one thing at a time; do not scatter your energies, nor leave something half done to begin a new venture. — Paramahansa Yogananda

What we do with our lives individually is not what determines whether we are a success or not. What determines whether we are a success is how we have affected the lives of others.

— Albert Schweitzer

Success on any major scale requires you to accept responsibility.... In the final analysis, the one quality that all successful people have... is the ability to take on responsibility.　　— Michael Korda

It is not enough to be busy, so are the ants. The question is, what are we busy about?

— Henry David Thoreau

I always advise young men who write me on the subject to do one thing well, throwing all their energies into it.

— John Wanamaker

To follow, without halt, one aim: There's the secret of success.　　— Anna Pavlova

There is only one success — to be able to spend your life your own way.   — Christopher Morley

Success follows doing what you want to do. There is no other way to be successful.

— Malcolm Forbes

Put your heart, mind, intellect and soul even to your smallest acts. This is the secret of success.

— Swami Sivananda

Everybody has barriers and obstacles.... If you look at them as hurdles that strengthen you each time you go over one, then you're going to be a success.

— Benjamin S. Carson

Silence and seclusion are the secrets of success. In this modern life of activity there is only one way to separate your self from its ceaseless demands: get away from it once in a while.

— Paramahansa Yogananda

Nothing can add more power to your life than concentrating all of your energies on a limited set of targets. — Nido Qubein

Striving for excellence motivates you; striving for perfection is demoralizing.
— Harriet Braiker

The secret of getting ahead is getting started.
— Sally Berger

If you have faith in yourself, and the amount of work you put into something, you're going to be successful eventually. — Steve Nash

Success is the sum of small efforts, repeated day in and day out. — Robert Collier

I know the price of success: dedication, hard work and an unremitting devotion to the things you want to see happen. — Frank Lloyd Wright

TRUTH

Truth is basically simple and feels good, clear and right.

— Chick Corea

All that is true, by whomsoever it has been said, has its origin in the Spirit.

— Thomas Aquinas

Truth is the only safe ground to stand upon.

— Elizabeth Cady Stanton

No man, for any considerable time, can wear one face to himself and another to the multitude without finally getting bewildered as to which may be the true.

— Nathaniel Hawthorne

VISION

If you can dream it, you can do it.
— Walt Disney

Whatever you can do or dream you can do, begin it. Boldness has genius, power and magic in it. Begin it now. — Johann Wolfgang von Goethe

Everything depends on execution; having just a vision is no solution. — Stephen Sondheim

The only limits are, as always, those of vision.
— James Broughton

Vision is the art of seeing things invisible.
— Jonathan Swift

WORK

1. Out of clutter, find simplicity.
2. From discord, find harmony.
3. In the middle of difficulty lies opportunity.
— Albert Einstein

I don't want to work for pay, but I want to be paid for my work. — Leonard Cohen

Throw yourself out into the convolutions of the world.... Take chances, make your own work, take pride in it. Seize the moment.
— Joan Didion

There is no future in any job — the future is in you.
— Napolean Hill & Dennis Kimbro

The value of achievement lies in the achieving.
— Albert Einstein

I'm a great believer in luck, and I find the harder I work the more I have of it.

— Thomas Edison

Sometimes the best deals are the ones you don't make.

— Bill Veeck

One of the symptoms of an approaching nervous breakdown is the belief that one's work is terribly important.

— Bertrand Russell

If (you're) going to sweep the floor, sweep it better than anybody in town. And if you're going to play the guitar, really, really, really get into it, and don't be jivin'.

— Carlos Santana

Fatigue is often caused not by work, but by worry, frustration and resentment. We rarely get tired when we are doing something interesting and exciting.

— Dale Carnegie

You can't grow if you're driven only by process, or only by the creative spirit. You've got to achieve a fragile balance between the two sides of the corporate brain. — Howard Schultz

Your work is to discover your work and then with all your heart to give yourself to it.
— Buddha

It is clear the future holds opportunities — it also holds pitfalls. The trick will be to seize the opportunities, avoid the pitfalls, and get back home by 6:00.
— Woody Allen

There are no shortcuts to any place worth going.
— Beverly Sills

I went back to being an amateur, in the sense of somebody who loves what she is doing. If a professional loses the love of work, routine sets in, and that's the death of work and of life.
— Ade Bethune

If you have love you will do all things well.

— Thomas Merton

During a very busy life I have often been asked, How did you manage to do it all? The answer is very simple — because I did everything promptly.

— Sir Richard Tangye

The key is to trust your heart to move where your talents can flourish. This old world will really spin when work becomes a joyous expression of the soul.

— Al Sacharov

To be successful, the first thing to do is fall in love with your work.   — Sister Mary Lauretta

To work in the world lovingly means that we are defining what we will be *for*, rather than reacting to what we are against.   — Christine Baldwin

If you continue to work and absorb the beauty in the world around you, you will find that age does not necessarily mean getting old.

— Pablo Casals

Always leave enough time in your life to do something that makes you happy, satisfied, even joyous. That has more of an effect on economic well-being than any other single factor.

— Paul Hawken

PERMISSIONS

Quotations by Paramahansa Yogananda appear courtesy of Self-Realization Fellowship and are credited as follows:

page 32, Paramahansa Yogananda quoted in *Spiritual Diary*;
page 96, from *Journey to Self-Realization* by Paramahansa Yogananda;
page 110, from *God Talks With Arjuna* by Paramahansa Yogananda;
page 123, from *Law of Success* by Paramahansa Yogananda;
page 127, from *The Divine Romance* by Paramahansa Yogananda;
page 134, from *Law of Success* by Paramahansa Yogananda;
page 136, from *The Divine Romance* by Paramahansa Yogananda;

all published by Self-Realization Fellowship, Los Angeles.

INDEX

About the Editor

Julian Ross has been on the search for the perfect quote since 1983, when he created *The Original Student Calendar* and needed to find a great quote every week. He lives with his family in the West Kootenay area of southeastern British Columbia where he works as a publisher and editor, and dreams of one day being able to fully live the truth of Thomas Edison's quotation: "There is time for everything."